CONTENTS

G000278725

Young Jesus — Day 1–4

A special job — Day 5–8

Love — Day 9–14

Moses, a great leader — Day 15–21

A man who cared — Day 22–27

Peace — Day 28–32

Elisha helps — Day 33–38

A little man — Day 39–47

Praising and thanks — Day 48–53

Abraham — Day 54–60

Luke 2 verse 41

Mary, Joseph and Jesus had to go to Jerusalem for a special celebration. Many people gathered in the city and sang, praised and prayed to God for all the good things He had done.

Talkabout — What special days do you like to celebrate and why?

Prayer — Dear Jesus, thank You that You give me special times to celebrate. Amen

Jesus and Me

and Me

Every Day

Eira Reeves

Book 2

Copyright © Eira Reeves 2009

Published 2009 by CWR, Waverley Abbey House, Waverley Lane, Farnham, Surrey GU9 8EP, UK.
Registered Charity No. 294387. Registered Limited Company No. 1990308.

The right of Eira Reeves to be identified as the author and illustrator of this work has been asserted
by her in accordance with the Copyright, Designs and Patents Act 1988, sections 77 and 78.

All rights reserved. No part of this publication may be reproduced, stored in a retrieval system,
or transmitted, in any form or by any means, electronic, mechanical, photocopying, recording or
otherwise, without the prior permission in writing of CWR.

For a list of our National Distributors, visit www.cwr.org.uk

Concept development, editing, design and production by CWR

Printed in Latvia by Yeomans Press

ISBN: 978-1-85345-519-3

After the celebration, Mary and Joseph were returning home, but Jesus went missing! Mary and Joseph were so very worried and started to search for Him everywhere.

Talkabout How do you think your parents or carers would feel if you went missing?

Prayer Dear Lord Jesus, please always keep me safe in Your care. Amen

A little later on Mary and Joseph found Jesus.
He wasn't harmed at all but was teaching
grown-ups in Jerusalem.
Jesus was only twelve years old!

Talkabout

Do you like Jesus as a teacher? Why?

Prayer

Thank You, Father God, for giving us Jesus so
that He can teach us. Amen

When Jesus was a little older, He helped Joseph in the carpenters shop. Each day Jesus would saw and hammer and make things out of wood.

Talkabout Look at the picture and say what tools carpenters use.

Prayer Dear God, thank You that You gave work to Jesus. Amen

Now Jesus knew that His heavenly Father God had a very special job for Him to do in the world. One day Jesus went to the River Jordan to see John (who we think was His cousin).

Talkabout

Do you have any cousins? Perhaps Mummy and Daddy have some? What are their names?

Prayer

Thank You, Jesus, for cousins everywhere. Amen

Cousin John was dipping people in the River Jordan and giving them new life. He looked up and saw Jesus coming and said, 'This man is far greater than anyone.'

Talkabout Why do you think Jesus is greater than anyone?

Prayer Dear Jesus, You are my hero and I think You're great! Amen

As John dipped Jesus in the water a dove could be seen above Jesus. This was the Holy Spirit. Now Jesus was ready for that special job that God had given Him.

Talkabout Dipping someone in the water as John did is called baptising. Do you know anyone who has been baptised or christened?

Prayer Thank You, God, that John baptised Jesus. Amen

After Jesus was baptised, He gathered some friends together to help Him with His special job.
'Come,' said Jesus, 'follow Me.' He wanted His friends to help Him.

Talkabout

Who are your best friends and why?

Prayer

Dear Jesus, thank You for giving friends to Jesus and me. Amen

'Wait,' said Mummy to Sue, 'I want you to tidy up your room, then you can go out and play with your friends.' Sue tidied her room but really she wanted to go out and play.

 **Talkabout** — Which do you think Jesus would prefer Sue to do, wait and help her mummy or to go out and play with friends?

Prayer — Thank You, Jesus, that You give us patience to wait. Amen

Kim was out for the day and one of his friends, John, went too.
John was in a wheelchair, so Kim helped to push him.
'Thank you for being so kind,' said John.

Talkabout Can you think of ways of being kind to help
other people?

Prayer Thank You, Jesus, that You are always kind.
Help me to be kind too. Amen

Love does not envy

Sarah's aunt had given her a present. It was a huge doll and it made Sarah feel very happy. Her friend Sue wished that she had been given a doll too.

Talkabout Have you ever wanted something that a friend had? Can you talk about it?

Prayer Dear Jesus, please teach me to be happy with the toys that I have already. Amen

1 Corinthians 13 verse 5

Love is not rude

One day, at school, David was playing with his friends. He was having such fun. Suddenly another boy came and pushed him. 'Hey,' said David, 'that's not nice.'

 Have you noticed anyone being rude? What happened?

 Dear Jesus, You don't like us being rude. Please teach me manners. Amen

Kelly's Mummy had bought her a new dress because she was going to a party. As Kelly walked into the room she said, 'Hello everyone, look at me, how do you like my dress?'

Talkabout

What do you think of Kelly saying this? How do you think she should have gone into the room?

Prayer

Dear Jesus, help me not to show off and make other people feel bad. Amen

Mummy wanted Sue to know just how much God loves each one of us.
'He gave us His Son Jesus,' she said to Sue, 'so that we may know how BIG His love is.'

 Do you know the love of Jesus? Say which ways you know His love.

Prayer Dear God, thank You that You gave us Jesus to show love. I love Jesus. Amen

One day, the Pharaoh's daughter, a princess, found a Hebrew baby amongst the rushes in a river. The baby was safely tucked up in a basket.
'Let's save him,' said the princess to her friends.

Talkabout The princess called the baby Moses. What is your favourite name?

Prayer Thank You, dear God, that You know each of us by name. Amen

Moses grew up to be a prince in a very grand palace in Egypt. But he was very sad because his people, the Hebrews, were used as slaves in the land. He thought this was unfair.

Talkabout

Have you ever seen anything that was unfair?

Prayer

Dear God, thank You that You helped Moses through this very bad time. Amen

Because he was sad Moses ran away from the palace into the country. He became a shepherd. One day a bush was on fire and an angel spoke to Moses from the flames.

Talkabout God was about to make Moses a leader. Do you know any leaders?

Prayer Dear God, thank You for all of our leaders today. Amen

Speaking to Pharaoh

'Go,' said the angel to Moses, 'and ask Pharaoh to let your people, the Hebrews, be set free.' After many days Pharaoh told all the Hebrew people to leave Egypt.

Talkabout Do you like asking people for things? Can you talk about it if you don't like asking?

Prayer Dear God, help me in times when I'm not too sure of something and need to ask. Amen

Moses led his people through
the desert to another
country far away.
On the way to this country
God gave Moses some rules
for His people.

Talkabout

These rules are called
the Ten Commandments.
What rules do your
family have?

Prayer

Thank You, dear God, for
showing us Your way to
live. Amen

An important rule

One of the rules from the Ten Commandments is that children should respect their parents. This is very important to God because He loves families.

Talkabout 'Respect' means 'admire'. What do you admire about your mummy and daddy?

 **Prayer** Thank You, God, for giving me my mummy and daddy. Help me to respect them. Amen

God's protection

Exodus 40 verse 38

Moses was a great leader and finally he led his people to the new land. All the way God had protected and guided them under a cloud through many difficult times.

 **Talkabout** Has God helped you through a difficult time? How?

Prayer Thank You, dear God, for seeing me through difficult times. Amen

'One day,' said Jesus, telling a story, 'a man was travelling from Jerusalem to Jericho. It was a long journey,' continued Jesus, 'and it was very hot and sandy.'

Talkabout Have you got an atlas? Try and find Jerusalem.

Prayer Dear Lord Jesus, I love it when You tell a story. Amen

On the way, robbers pounced on the man. They bullied and fought him and took all his money. The poor traveller was left very hurt.

Talkabout Sometimes bullies push people around. Have you seen someone bullied? Can you talk about it?

Prayer Dear Jesus, please will You protect me and my friends. Amen

Luke 10 verse 30

The traveller lay on the ground in the hot sunshine. He had been badly hurt. The robbers had left him to die from his wounds. There was no one around to help him.

Talkabout What do you think is bad about these robbers?

Prayer Dear Jesus, You know when robbers do bad things. Help them to be good. Amen

Some time later, a man was passing by and saw the poor traveller on the ground. He noticed that he was suffering so he stopped to help him.

Talkabout

Suffering can make you very miserable. Do you know anyone helping those people who are suffering?

Prayer

Dear Jesus, thank You for this man who stopped and helped the man who was suffering. Amen

The man bandaged the traveller's wounds. He then put the
traveller on his donkey and set off on a long journey to find
a hotel.

Talkabout What do you think about the man who
bandaged the wounds of the traveller?

Prayer Dear God, thank You for kind people who stop
and help. Amen

At last the man found a hotel.
'Here is some money,' the helping man said to the manager of the hotel, 'please look after this poor wounded man until he's better.'

Talkabout

What do you like about this story?

Prayer

Thank You, Jesus, for showing us about kindness. Amen

Jesus is known as the Prince of Peace and if we want peace we need to look to Jesus.
Jesus used to go away to places of peace to talk to His heavenly Father.

Talkabout

Where do you go to when you want to find some peace?

Prayer

Dear Jesus, thank You for Your peace. Amen

'Mummy!' yelled Ben, 'I can't sleep.' So Mummy went into his bedroom. 'Let's read a book about Jesus,' she said.
After his mummy had read a story to him Ben slept very peacefully.

Talkabout Can you talk about the times when you can't sleep and why?

Prayer Dear Jesus, thank You that You are with me when I lie down to go to sleep. Amen

'Please will you pray for me, Sue,' cried Kelly. 'Kim has just shouted at me and I'm upset.'
Immediately Sue prayed for Kelly so that she would know the peace of Jesus.

Talkabout Has this happened to you? Did you ask someone to pray with you?

 Dear Jesus, thank You that when we are hurt You can give us peace. Amen

'Stop it!' said Mummy. 'Don't quarrel please.'
Sue and Max had been fighting over the last biscuit on the plate. Mummy was trying to bring peace between them.

Talkabout Have you ever been a peacemaker between friends? What happened?

Prayer Dear Jesus, help me to be a peacemaker when there is trouble. Amen

It was Max's first day at school and Mummy was going to take him. But before they left home Mummy sat down and prayed with Max because he was a little worried.

Do you ever pray when you are worried?

Dear Jesus, let me know Your peace when I am worried. Amen

Now there was a man called Naaman. He was a leader of the army and he was a very strong man.
But one day Naaman became ill with a skin disease.

Talkabout

Can you pray for someone who is ill? What is their name?

Prayer

Dear God, I pray for
..........Daddy.Darren.........Please make them better. Amen

him

her

'Elisha will help Namaan,' said a servant girl to Naaman's wife. 'He will help him to get better and strong again.'

Talkabout How would you like to help someone today or tomorrow?

 **Prayer** Thank You, dear God, for Elisha wanting to help Namaan. Amen

God showed Elisha what was best for Naaman. God wanted Naaman healed and well as He only wanted the best for him.

Talkabout

God wants the best for you. Do you know why?

Prayer

Dear God, I'm so glad that You love me so much that You want the best for me. Amen

'Go and tell Naaman to bathe in the river,' said Elisha to the servant girl. But when Naaman was told this he became angry. He didn't think he should do this as he was a great leader.

Talkabout Have you ever felt you didn't want to do something? Why?

Prayer Dear God, help me to do as I am told. Amen

Naaman didn't know God so he didn't want to listen to Elisha telling him what to do. 'Please Naaman,' encouraged his servants, 'go and bathe in the river.'

 Talkabout 'Encourage' means 'support'. Who would you like to encourage?

Prayer Dear God, show me how to encourage friends day by day. Amen

So Naaman went into the river. After a little while he came out and looked at his skin. It was totally clear. 'WOW,' shouted Namaan. 'I've been healed. Now I believe in God!'

Talkabout Do you know anyone who doesn't believe in God? Can you tell them about Jesus?

Prayer Please Jesus, help me to speak to those who don't know You. Amen

One day Jesus went to a town called Jericho. The crowds were so excited to see Jesus in their town.
But Zacchaeus, who was very small, couldn't see over the crowds.

Talkabout What is the name of your city/town/village?
What do you like about it?

Prayer Today, I pray for every person who lives in my city/town/village. Amen

Now Zacchaeus was a very important tax collector. That meant people had to give him a lot of money, but sometimes he took money he wasn't meant to. He was dishonest.

Talkabout — Dishonest means not doing something right. What would you do if someone was dishonest?

Prayer — Dear Lord Jesus, please always help everyone to do things right. Amen

Zacchaeus climbed a tree so that he could see Jesus. Up and up he climbed till he reached the top of the tree. He could now see Jesus and he was so excited!

 **Talkabout** What makes you excited and why?

 **Prayer** Dear Jesus, thank You that You love us to be excited about You. Amen

When Jesus reached the tree where Zacchaeus was He looked up and said, 'Climb down from that tree, Zacchaeus. I want to visit you and stay in your home.'

Talkabout

If you had an invitation from Jesus what would be the first thing you would do?

Prayer

Dear Jesus, You knew all about Zacchaeus but You still wanted to be with him. Amen

Zacchaeus scrambled down the tree. He had an invitation from Jesus. How wonderful! Jesus was SO important and he didn't want to miss this invitation.

If Jesus called you today what would you say?

Dear Jesus, I'm so glad that You are important to me.
Amen

Luke 19 verse 7

The crowd were unhappy when they saw Jesus call Zacchaeus.
'Why?' they said. 'This man is a cheat and Jesus has given him
an invite. That's not right!'

Talkabout What do you think about this? Do you think it
is right or wrong?

 Dear Jesus, even though Zacchaeus was a
cheat, You wanted to change his heart. Amen

Zacchaeus was so very pleased to get an invite from Jesus and he was so proud to be walking with Him. 'I want to give something back,' said Zacchaeus to Jesus.

 **Talkabout** What would you like to give Jesus?

Prayer Dear Jesus, I give You my heart today. Thank You that I can walk with You. Amen

'I'm so sorry I have cheated people with their money, I will give it all back to them,' Zacchaeus said to Jesus, 'and also I will give half my money to the poor.'

Talkabout Do you think Jesus was pleased with Zacchaeus? Why?

Prayer

Thank You, dear Jesus, for touching Zacchaeus' heart. Amen

'I'm so sorry,' cried Zacchaeus to Jesus, 'for all the bad things I have done.' 'Zacchaeus,' replied Jesus, 'I forgive you.' Zacchaeus was so happy with these words.

 **Talkabout** When you have done something wrong do you find it easy or hard to say sorry?

Prayer Dear Jesus, help me to say sorry when I am in the wrong. Amen

'Today,' said Mrs Brown the playgroup leader, 'I'm going to tell you a story about Jesus.' Afterwards all the friends danced to music praising Jesus.

Talkabout 'Praise' means 'to give thanks'. How do you like to praise Jesus?

Prayer Dear Jesus, I always want to praise and sing to You. Amen

'Come on,' said Daddy to Sarah, Ben and David. 'It's time to go to church.' They all loved to go to church, as they learnt about Jesus, sang songs, prayed and thanked Him.

 Which is your favourite song and why?

Prayer Dear God, thank You that I can praise You always. Amen

'Let's go to the wildlife park,' said Mummy. 'I want to show you all the flowers, birds and butterflies and spiders.' Sue and her friends were very excited.

Talkabout
Don't you think God's work is beautiful? How would you like to say thank You?

Prayer
Dear God, I love all the things You have made in this world. Thank You. Amen

'Soon you will have a baby sister,' said Mummy to Kelly. 'Even now,' continued Mummy patting her tummy, 'your baby sister is safe in the care of God.'

Talkabout

What do you think about God knowing you before you were born?

Prayer

Thank You, dear God, that You knew me all the time and kept me safe before I was born. Amen

Sarah had been at playgroup all morning. She saw her daddy waiting and ran towards him.
'Hello Daddy,' she yelled, 'I'm so pleased to see you.' Daddy gave her a big, big hug.

Talkabout   Describe what it's like to be hugged by someone who loves you.

Prayer   Thank You, God, that Your arms are always around me keeping me safe. Amen

Kim was having a birthday party. He was so excited because all his family, including his cousins, and friends were coming and he was looking forward to being with them all.

Talkabout How do you feel when all your family and friends get together?

Prayer I want to sing Your praises, Jesus, for all my family and friends. Amen

There was a man called Abraham and he had a wife called Sarah. 'Pack up,' said God to Abraham one day, 'and I will show you a new country.'

Talkabout Do you enjoy packing your bags when you go away? What do you pack?

Prayer Thank You, God, for always being with us when we go away. Amen

Abraham gathered his family together. They did a lot of packing and put all their belongings on camels and donkeys. Then Abraham and his family set off.

 **Talkabout**

What do you like about a new adventure?

Prayer

Thank You, God, that Abraham set off not knowing where he was going, but he trusted You. Amen

Then God spoke to Abraham again. 'You are going to have a son.' Abraham was so happy with this news, even though he and Sarah were very, very, very old!

Talkabout How old do you think the people who take care of you are?

 Prayer Thank You, God, that whatever age we are, we are always important to You. Amen

Abraham found it difficult to believe that God would give him and Sarah a baby. But God had given His promise. 'You are to call the baby Isaac,' said God to Abraham.

Talkabout

'Isaac' means 'he laughs'. Perhaps you can find out what your name means.

Prayer

Thank You, God, that You know us all by name. Amen

'Look up at the sky,' said God to Abraham, 'someday your family will be bigger than all the stars in the sky.'
That's an awfully BIG family to have!

Talkabout

Have you ever tried to count the stars in the sky. What number did you get up to?

Prayer

Thank You, God, for Abraham, his family and for stars! Amen

Genesis 20 verses 14–16

God blessed Abraham and
Sarah with many things,
like hundreds of animals
and lots of gold and silver.
Abraham became
God's friend.

Talkabout

What blessings has God given you?

Prayer

Thank You, God, that You love
to bless us. Thank You for my
blessings today. Amen

Time went by and then, just as God had promised, He gave Abraham and Sarah a baby in their old age. They called him Isaac and they were all very happy.

 Have you ever promised something to someone? What was it?

Prayer Dear God, help me to keep promises just as You always do. Amen

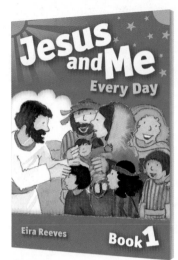

Sixty more beautifully illustrated daily devotionals by Eira Reeves, for 3- to 6-year-olds:

- In the very beginning
- Another special plan
- Giving
- Noah
- Jesus and children
- David the shepherd
- A huge picnic
- Helping
- Jonah

£5.99
ISBN: 978-1-85345-518-6

For when you're too old for Jesus and Me Every Day

Topz helps 7- to 11-year-olds get to know God and His Word through an exciting, day-by-day look at the Bible. Daily Bible readings and simple prayers are augmented by readers' contributions along with fun and colourful word games, puzzles and cartoons.

£13.80 UK annual subscription (6 issues)
Individual copies also available: £2.49 each
72-page, full-colour booklet, 210x148mm, published bimonthly
ISSN: 0967-1307

Visit **www.cwr.org.uk** or call **01252 78471052**
Prices correct at time of printing.